The *Untold Story*
of the
Battle of
Saratoga
A Turning Point in the Revolutionary War

by Michael Burgan

COMPASS POINT BOOKS
a capstone imprint

Compass Point Books are published by Capstone,
1710 Roe Crest Drive, North Mankato, Minnesota 56003
www.capstonepub.com

Editorial Credits
Jennifer Huston, editor; Heidi Thompson, designer;
Eric Gohl, media researcher; Laura Manthe, production specialist;
Kathleen Baxter, library consultant

Special thanks to Joseph Craig, Interpretive Park Ranger at Saratoga National
Historic Park, for serving as content adviser.

Photo Credits
Alamy: North Wind Picture Archives, cover, 27, 42, 55, 57, Universal Images
Group Limited, 9; Andy Thomas, Artist, Battle of Saratoga—Revolutionary
War: 41; Courtesy of Army Art Collection, U.S. Army Center of Military
History: 32; Bridgeman Images: British Library, London, UK, 12, © Look
and Learn/Private Collection, 6, 29; Getty Images: Fotosearch, 21, Stock
Montage, 52, UIG/Prisma, 10, Universal History Archive, 5; Glow Images:
SuperStock, 24, 51; Library of Congress: 23, 49; Courtesy of Saratoga
National Historical Park, National Park Service: 30, 38; United States Military
Academy: Department of History, 16; Wikimedia: Public Domain, 8, 15;
www.historicalimagebank.com, Painting by Don Troiani: 43; Yale University
Art Gallery: 18

Design Elements: Shutterstock

Library of Congress Cataloging-in-Publication Data
Burgan, Michael.
   The Untold Story of the Battle of Saratoga : A Turning Point in the
Revolutionary War/by Michael Burgan.
      pages cm.—What You Didn't Know about the American Revolution
   Includes bibliographical references and index.
   ISBN 978-0-7565-4974-9 (library binding)
   ISBN 978-0-7565-4978-7 (paperback)
   ISBN 978-0-7565-4982-4 (ebook PDF)
   1. Saratoga Campaign, N.Y., 1777—Juvenile literature. I. Title.

E241.S2B86 2015
973.3'33—dc23   2014031845

Printed in the United States of America in Stevens Point, Wisconsin.
092014   008479WZS15

TABLE OF
Contents

CHAPTER *One*

A Decisive Time

Inside his quarters in upstate New York, Major General Benedict Arnold heard the sounds of war all around him. He wanted to be out on the battlefield leading his men against the British once again. He had fought bravely several weeks before during a battle at nearby Freeman's Farm. But Arnold had bitterly quarreled with his commanding officer, Major General Horatio Gates, who was in charge of the entire Northern Army. When the second Battle of Saratoga began, Gates ordered Arnold to stay at the camp.

But as muskets fired and cannons roared, Arnold couldn't stand it anymore. He borrowed a horse and rushed off to the battle. He would once again lead American troops in their fight for freedom and independence from British rule. Arnold had no idea that this would be a turning point in the fighting and one of the most important battles of the Revolutionary War.

Benedict Arnold fought courageously at the Battle of Saratoga.

A Difficult War

The two battles collectively known as the Battle of Saratoga were fought September 19 and October 7, 1777. By then the Revolutionary War had been going strong for more than two years. The patriots were struggling against the much larger and better-trained British Army. Back in March 1776, the British had pulled out of Boston, the scene of the first major fighting. But then they sent 30,000 troops to capture New York City.

During a series of battles that summer, the British won several key victories to seize control of New York City and the

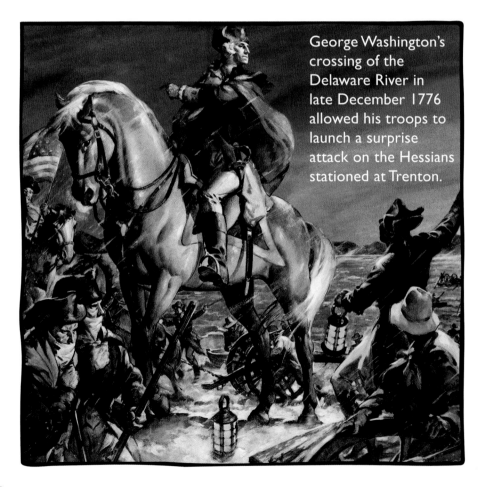

George Washington's crossing of the Delaware River in late December 1776 allowed his troops to launch a surprise attack on the Hessians stationed at Trenton.

surrounding area. In December 1776 General George Washington wrote to his cousin Lund expressing the problems his Continental army faced: "…your imagination can scarce extend to a situation more distressing than mine."

The first hint of hope for Washington came December 26, 1776, when American forces at Trenton, New Jersey, surprised and captured hundreds of Hessian soldiers who were fighting for the British. Another American victory came the following week at nearby Princeton. A loyalist wrote that the patriots had been losing faith in the cause, but the two victories made them "all liberty mad again."

These American victories were short lived, however, and Washington's problems soon returned. In early 1777 the Continental army had roughly 3,000 men. Washington pleaded with the states to send militia to help his full-time soldiers, but the states had trouble recruiting men to fight. In addition, the Continental Congress was struggling to pay its bills as it fought a war that seemed as if it might drag on forever.

Help from the Hessians

The Germans who fought for the British during the Revolutionary War were referred to as Hessians. About two-thirds of them came from the German state of Hesse-Cassel, which is how they got their nickname. But soldiers from other small German states also helped the British. Most Germans who fought at Saratoga came from Braunschweig, which the British called Brunswick.

A Grand Plan

In early 1777 British Lieutenant General John Burgoyne proposed an invasion of New York from Canada along Lake Champlain and the Hudson River. If Burgoyne's plan worked, the British would control the Hudson River Valley. New England, to the east, would also be cut off from the other colonies.

John Burgoyne

Burgoyne hoped this would force the Americans to surrender, thus winning the war for the British.

To put his plan into play, Burgoyne organized about 10,000 troops. The force under his command would sail south across Lake Champlain, which stretches into Quebec, Canada, from New York and Vermont. After that Burgoyne's troops would march south along the Hudson River to Albany, New York.

Meanwhile, a smaller British force under the command of Lieutenant Colonel Barry St. Leger would leave from Fort Oswego, along Lake Ontario in New York, and advance to the southeast. These troops would act as a diversion, forcing the patriots to send soldiers to stop them. The British expected to defeat the Americans and continue on to Albany.

Burgoyne's Proposed Invasion

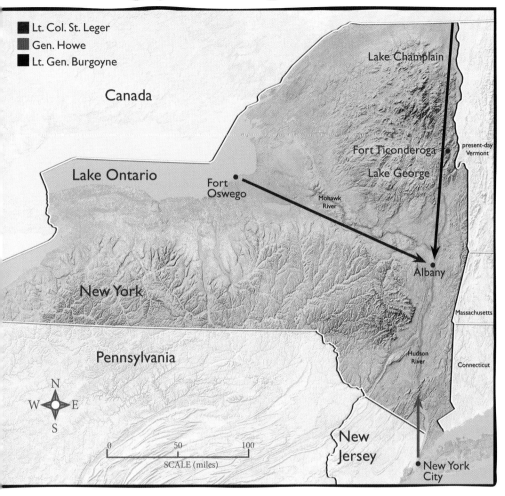

Burgoyne also hoped that British General William Howe would march his troops north from New York City, and the three armies would combine to defeat the patriots in New England. But Howe was unwilling to commit to that part of the plan.

"I look upon America as our child, which we have already spoilt by too much indulgence."

—John Burgoyne, speaking in Parliament in 1774

Help from Abroad

While Burgoyne was in London in early 1777 seeking King George's support for his plan, Benjamin Franklin was on a similar mission in France for the patriots. As a U.S. diplomat living in Paris, Franklin was trying to convince King Louis XVI to send aid to the Americans.

France and Great Britain had been enemies for centuries. But France did not want to declare war on Great Britain unless the Americans seemed certain of winning their independence on the battlefield. Even so, the French wanted to help.

Benjamin Franklin (left) met with France's King Louis XVI to persuade him to help the Americans win their independence from Great Britain.

Beginning in 1776 France unofficially sent money through a fake trading company that sent weapons and supplies to the Americans. In addition, four ships were filled with supplies and ready to sail to America. However, when Louis XVI heard about the American losses in New York in the summer of 1776, he ordered the ships to remain in port.

But when Washington scored successes at Trenton and Princeton in December, the French were again eager to help. In early 1777 the four ships carrying supplies left for the United States. The Americans quickly realized that the more successful they were on the battlefield, the more aid they could expect from France.

Did You Know?

The British and the loyalists liked the year 1777—or at least the figures in it. The three 7s resembled a row of gallows—the wooden frames used to hang people. The British hoped that the patriot leaders—whom they considered traitors—would soon be swinging from real gallows. They referred to 1777 as "the year of the hangman."

CHAPTER *Two*

The British Are Coming!

Ships carrying additional British and German troops joined forces with troops already based in Quebec. Burgoyne's ship reached Canada on May 6, 1777. Major General Friedrich Adolph Riedesel led most of the 3,000 or so German troops in Burgoyne's army. Other key officers included Brigadier General Simon Fraser and Major General William Phillips.

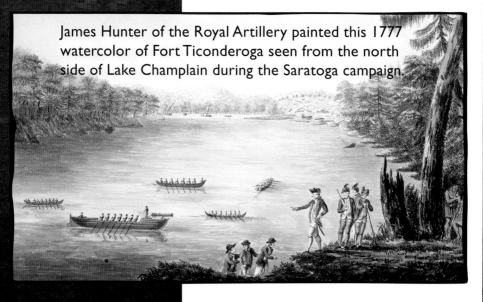

James Hunter of the Royal Artillery painted this 1777 watercolor of Fort Ticonderoga seen from the north side of Lake Champlain during the Saratoga campaign.

By late June Burgoyne and the 7,000 men under his command headed south toward New York. Fewer loyalists, Canadians, and American Indians had chosen to take part than he had hoped. But as always, Burgoyne was sure of the skills of his trained soldiers. He moved out with confidence, writing that he was "determined to strike where necessary."

Burgoyne set his sites on Fort Ticonderoga, which was located on the southern end of Lake Champlain in New York. The Americans had taken the fort from the British in May 1775 and began to strengthen some of its defenses by placing guns on a nearby hill.

Inside the fort, Major General Arthur St. Clair was growing increasingly nervous. He knew of Burgoyne's arrival in Canada and assumed those forces would sail for New York City. But activity nearby hinted that the British were heading his way. If Burgoyne and his troops did move south, St. Clair knew that Fort Ticonderoga would be their first target.

Henry Knox: A Man on a Mission

The capture of Fort Ticonderoga in 1775 had provided important weapons for the Continental army. Boston was in danger of being seized by the British, and the Americans were in desperate need of weapons. So Henry Knox suggested a plan to haul the weapons from Fort Ticonderoga to Boston. General George Washington liked the idea, so he ordered Knox to put the plan into action. During the difficult mission, Knox and his men used sleds and oxen to transport the artillery more than 300 miles (483 kilometers) across frozen lakes and rivers, rugged mountains, and snowy countryside.

Preparing a Defense

By June 1777 troops at Fort Ticonderoga were building another fort on a neighboring hill known as Mount Independence. But even with those improvements, St. Clair did not feel that he had enough men to hold off an invading army. Plus the men he did have lacked proper weapons. Because some had no bayonets, they would have to use sharpened poles during hand-to-hand combat. Clothing and food were also scarce.

St. Clair also had another problem: He was unsure what Burgoyne was up to. St. Clair thought that the British were close because in the woods near the fort, his scouts had confronted American Indians who were aiding the British. He believed that the Indians would not have moved so freely around the fort if they did not have help nearby. But St. Clair had no way of knowing how many enemy troops might be advancing or where they intended to strike. They could head west into New York's Mohawk Valley or east into New Hampshire.

Did You Know?

Burgoyne told the Indians who fought for him that they could take scalps from the Americans they killed in battle. He also promised to pay them for any prisoners they captured. An Iroquois chief assured Burgoyne that the Indians would be obedient to the "great father beyond the great lake"—King George III.

Major General Arthur St. Clair was in charge of Fort Ticonderoga during the summer of 1777.

Overwhelmed by uncertainty, St. Clair wrote to Major General Philip Schuyler that "No army was ever in a more critical situation than we now are."

Finally on June 30, soldiers at Fort Ticonderoga could see British ships on Lake Champlain. As the British began coming ashore, some of them fought in a skirmish with the Americans. St. Clair's forces captured one of them. The prisoner revealed the size of Burgoyne's army, which St. Clair now realized with certainty was coming for Fort Ticonderoga.

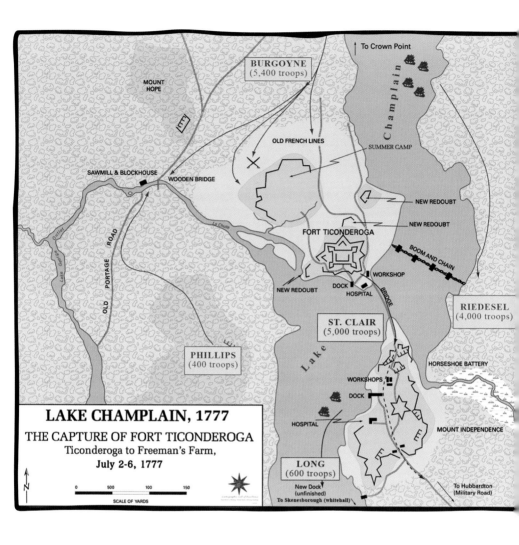

LAKE CHAMPLAIN, 1777

THE CAPTURE OF FORT TICONDEROGA
Ticonderoga to Freeman's Farm,
July 2-6, 1777

SCALE OF YARDS
0   500   100   150

Leaving a Fort Behind

Not only was St. Clair outnumbered, soon he was also outmaneuvered. A large hill known as Mount Defiance overlooked Fort Ticonderoga. American generals had discussed positioning artillery on it as they had on other hills, but nothing had been done. The hill seemed almost impossible to climb, much less drag heavy artillery up it.

Even so, on July 5 Burgoyne's men were able to haul several cannons up the hill and aim them at Fort Ticonderoga. Even worse, the British had enough troops that they could attack Mount Independence at the same time.

Rather than risk a battle he probably could not win, St. Clair ordered his men to leave the fort. They retreated to Mount Independence and then marched through the woods to Hubbardton, Vermont. Some of the troops also traveled south by boat. A few of the men grumbled about leaving Fort Ticonderoga without putting up a fight, but they lacked the knowledge St. Clair had about the size of Burgoyne's much larger army.

Burgoyne did not want to let the enemy get away, so soon the retreating Americans came under attack. British ships on South Bay, just below Lake Champlain, fired on the small American boats at Skenesborough, about 30 miles (48 km) south of Fort Ticonderoga. The Americans came ashore and began heading for Fort Ann, about 12 miles (19 km) away.

Meanwhile, St. Clair's land retreat continued to Hubbardton and then on to Castleton, Vermont. St. Clair kept some forces in Hubbardton as a rear guard, and they soon faced the British and Hessian soldiers who had been pursuing them. At the Battle of Hubbardton, the patriots offered stiff resistance, killing or wounding more than 150 enemy soldiers. But they suffered heavy losses, with 40 dead and about 90 wounded. As the battle ended, the surviving Americans retreated into the woods.

The next day, July 8, another battle took place outside Fort Ann. As American soldiers darted from tree to tree advancing on the British, their heavy, accurate fire forced the British to retreat. Just as the British were about to surrender, what sounded like an Indian war cry shrieked across the woods. This convinced the patriots that the enemy's fierce Indian allies were about to enter the battle. As a result, the Americans set fire to Fort Ann and retreated to Fort Edward.

However, what the Americans heard during the fighting that day was not really an Indian war cry. British Captain John Money could not convince the Indian warriors to fight the Americans in the woods. So he imitated an Indian war cry in an attempt to scare off the Americans—and it worked.

Several days later, St. Clair and his surviving men—around 1,500 soldiers—reached Fort Edward, about 12 miles (19 km) southwest of Fort Ann. Major General Philip Schuyler, commander of the Northern Army, was based at Fort Edward, which was the main American fort in the region. Schuyler had to decide what to do about Burgoyne's advancing forces.

Major General Philip Schuyler

The Death of Jane McCrea

During his slow march to Fort Edward, Burgoyne faced another problem. Some of the American Indians under his command disobeyed orders and attacked civilians. The incident that drew the most attention was the slaying of Jane McCrea.

McCrea's brother was in the New York militia, but her sweetheart was a loyalist who was fighting for Burgoyne. While attempting to meet up with her love, Jane was captured, shot, and then scalped.

News of Jane's murder spread throughout the region, shocking and angering many people. It turned many people against the British and aided the patriot cause by sparking a new wave of recruits to enlist.

One of Schuyler's first moves was to slow down the British. Most of Burgoyne's army was traveling by land toward Fort Edward, so Schuyler had his men destroy bridges and cut down trees to block the road. These actions delayed the British considerably—in three weeks they advanced only about 23 miles (37 km).

When the British finally reached Fort Edward on July 30, it was empty. Schuyler and his force of about 4,500 men had pulled out, thinking they could not defend the fort. They headed south about 23 miles (37 km) to Stillwater, New York.

An Important Victory

By this time George Washington had moved his troops out of New Jersey and into New York. They camped in the Hudson Highlands, a mountainous region north of New York City. Washington suspected that Burgoyne was moving south from Canada and that perhaps Howe was heading out of New York City to connect with Burgoyne. Washington was surprised, however, when he learned on July 24 that Howe and most of his army had sailed out of New York Harbor. Washington spent a few nerve-racking days trying to figure out where Howe was going. Once Howe sailed into Chesapeake Bay, Washington realized that Philadelphia—the capital of the United States at the

time—was the target. Washington prepared his men to march there.

Howe's decision to attack Philadelphia threatened Burgoyne's grand plan for the New York campaign. Howe had no plans to attack the capital and also help Burgoyne. He did leave a small force behind to defend New York City, but those troops were not numerous enough to aid

Burgoyne. Even without Howe's help, Burgoyne was ready to push on. However, he was counting on Colonel Barry St. Leger's troops from the west to meet up with him in Albany.

Like Burgoyne, St. Leger's force included more than 1,500 Germans, American Indians, Canadians, and loyalists. On August 3 they began a siege of Fort Schuyler (previously called Fort Stanwix), which is located in present-day Rome, New York. About 800 Americans defended the fort, which had been renamed the year before to honor Major General Schuyler. On August 6 the Americans learned that an additional 800 New York militiamen were on their way to help.

Fort Stanwix was built by the British during the French and Indian War (1754–1763), but it was abandoned after the war ended. American troops took it over in 1776 and renamed it Fort Schuyler. The fort was not rebuilt after a fire in 1781.

But those New York militiamen never reached Fort Schuyler. St. Leger knew they were coming and sent troops to ambush them. In a fierce fight called the Battle of Oriskany, the British and their Mohawk and Seneca allies wiped out more than half of the American soldiers. The survivors retreated, and the siege dragged on.

Major General Schuyler learned about the siege at Fort Schuyler and ordered Benedict Arnold to lead reinforcements there. St. Leger heard about the advancing American forces, but the situation had changed. The Indians he relied on so heavily were now less eager to fight. And St. Leger didn't know the exact size of Arnold's army. Rather than risk defeat, he pulled back. The Americans had saved the fort.

During the siege of Fort Schuyler, the Americans scored another victory east of there. Burgoyne sent troops—mostly Germans, loyalists, and American Indians under Colonel Friedrich Baum—to Bennington, Vermont,

Did You *Know?*

Benedict Arnold saved Fort Schuyler with some clever trickery. He promised that he would spare the life of a captured loyalist named Hon Yost Schuyler (who was a distant relative of American Major General Philip Schuyler) if he followed Arnold's orders. The prisoner was friendly with some of the local American Indians, so Arnold had him tell them that the patriots were nearby with a huge force. Rather than face this "massive" army, St. Leger's Indian allies deserted. St. Leger could not risk a fight without their help, so he retreated.

Fought on August 6, 1777, the Battle of Oriskany, was one of the bloodiest battles of the Revolutionary War.

to steal supplies. On August 16 about 8 miles (13 km) outside of Bennington, an American force of about 1,500 pounced on them in a surprise attack.

The Americans were led by General John Stark, who said the fighting sounded like "one continued clap of thunder."

The enemy forces had set up breastworks on a couple of nearby hills. Stark divided up his men and surrounded the larger hill. Then the patriots attacked from all sides.

Stark's men overran Baum's fortifications, capturing many soldiers as they fled down the hills. Several hundred German reinforcements arrived too late to save their comrades, but they still tried to save the day for the British. Fortunately for the Americans, their own reinforcements appeared—about 400 Continental army soldiers and Vermont militia members. With their arrival the Americans regained control of the battle, and the Germans soon retreated.

When the Battle of Bennington was over, Stark wrote in a letter to Horatio Gates that they killed 207 men and took about 700 prisoners, but the number of wounded was unknown. He also said that the Americans had lost 30 men with about 40 wounded.

After Bennington, several American officers happily noted

During the Battle of Bennington, General John Stark led about 1,600 militiamen in a victory over the professional British soldiers.

A North American Indian Civil War

Like the British, the Americans had Indian allies during the Saratoga campaign. The six main tribes of the region were collectively known as the Iroquois. They had made an agreement among themselves to help each other in times of war. But the Revolutionary War divided the Iroquois. This split has been referred to as a civil war.

Most members of the Oneida and Tuscarora tribes supported the Americans. The Mohawks, Cayugas, Onondagas, and Senecas joined the British. In 1779 American forces destroyed several villages of the Iroquois who helped the British. In retaliation, the tribes who supported the British destroyed Oneida and Tuscarora villages. After the war, most of the Iroquois who helped the British lost their land and resettled in Canada. The Oneida and Tuscarora received some money from the U.S. government for their losses, but it was not enough to rebuild their communities. Most ended up selling their land and moving to other states.

that Burgoyne had lost some of his confidence. And he had reason to because the state governors were sending more militiamen to confront him. In addition, Burgoyne lost most of his Indian warriors who had decided that it was no longer in their best interest to continue the fight and returned to their homes. His army also needed supplies, which Burgoyne could not get from the surrounding hostile countryside. Despite these challenges, Burgoyne decided to push on toward Albany, hoping that Howe would find a way to send troops to help him.

Gates in Charge

After the fall of Fort Ticonderoga, Congress had lost confidence in General Schuyler, so Major General Horatio Gates took command of the Northern Army. To Gates, this was his chance to prove his skills on the battlefield. Although he was cautious, Gates was known as a good planner and organizer. Some people also saw him as ambitious—eager to seek glory for himself whenever he could. Gates pushed hard to get command of the Northern Army so he could prove his skills.

When Gates took command in August 1777, the Northern Army was in bad shape. Morale was low, and the men lacked food and supplies. When Gates began placing orders to get them what they needed, the mood of the camp quickly improved.

When Gates arrived at Van Schaick's Island—where the Mohawk River meets the Hudson, about 40 miles (64 km) south of Burgoyne's camp at Fort Edward—he had about 6,000 troops. During late August and early September, more soldiers joined his ranks. Benedict Arnold arrived from Fort Schuyler with about 1,200 men. Then Colonel Daniel Morgan arrived with another 400, and George Washington sent Gates another 1,500 Continental soldiers. More militia would also answer the call to fight Burgoyne.

Gates' army of about 9,000 men began marching north on September 8. They eventually settled on hills overlooking the Hudson River known as Bemis Heights. Under the direction of Polish engineer Thaddeus Kosciuszko, the Americans built breastworks

Major General Horatio Gates

measuring more than 2 miles (3.2 km) long. Gates was content to stay at Bemis Heights and wait for Burgoyne to come to him. He did not have to wait long.

CHAPTER *Three*

Freeman's Farm:
The First Battle
of Saratoga

Burgoyne and his troops left Fort Edward in early September, ready to engage the Americans in battle. On the way Burgoyne learned from American deserters that Gates' army had set up a well-defended position at Bemis Heights near the town of Saratoga. He also heard that he was outnumbered by perhaps several thousand men. Still, he was preparing to attack.

Early on September 18, a company of men led by Benedict Arnold set out north of Bemis Heights to scout the region. They spotted a group of British soldiers on their hands and knees digging up potatoes in a field known as Freeman's Farm. The land was only about a mile (1.6 km) or so away from the American camp. Intent on finding food, the British soldiers didn't even realize they were being watched.

Arnold and his men took the potato diggers completely by surprise. The patriots charged them, killing or wounding 20 and capturing even more, while the rest fled back to Burgoyne's camp. The British general was close enough to see Arnold's men through his spyglass, but he did not strike. His plan was to wait until the next morning and then move west of the Americans and position his men on hills overlooking Bemis Heights. From there, the big guns could fire down onto Gates and his men.

The bloody battles of Saratoga were a turning point for the Americans.

The Armies Meet

Fog covered the ground around Bemis Heights on the morning of September 19, as drummers in both the British and American camps called the men to order. The two enemies were so close that each side could hear the other's drums. American scouts along the Hudson saw and heard activity in Burgoyne's camp. It was clear that the British were preparing for battle.

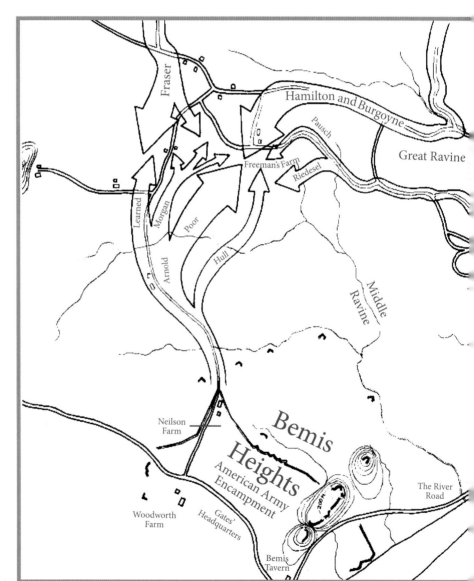

When General Gates received this news, he did not immediately plan to meet the advancing enemy. He was content to let Burgoyne come to him. But Arnold insisted that the proper strategy was to go out and meet the British.

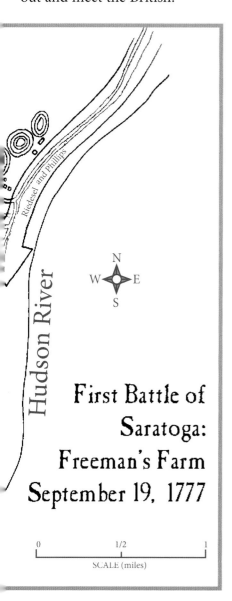

Hudson River

First Battle of Saratoga: Freeman's Farm September 19, 1777

Riedesel and Phillips

N
W · E
S

0   1/2   1
SCALE (miles)

If the Americans fought and were defeated at their lines, the result could be a disaster for them. If they fought away from the fortifications, they had the fortifications to retreat to. Gates allowed Arnold to send Colonel Daniel Morgan's 400 riflemen and 250 men from Major Henry Dearborn's Light Infantry. Gates also said Arnold could send out more of his men if Morgan's troops needed support.

Morgan's men set out north of the American camp to meet Burgoyne's army head on. Burgoyne had divided his forces into three columns to approach the American positions. Brigadier General Simon Fraser commanded the western column; Brigadier General James Hamilton, accompanied by Burgoyne, was in the center; and Major General Friedrich Riedesel had the eastern column closest to the Hudson River.

A group of Morgan's men positioned themselves near Freeman's Farm. Some went inside an abandoned log cabin, while others hid behind fences. Soon an advance party from Hamilton's forces approached, unaware of the American presence. When the British were in range, Morgan's men opened fire. The survivors retreated and some more were shot by their own men who mistook them for pursuing Americans. The rest of Morgan's and Dearborn's troops arrived at the farm only to be forced away by men arriving from Fraser's column to the west. The British killed some of Morgan's riflemen and captured several others.

Morgan and his men might have faced certain defeat at that point, except for one thing: Worried that Morgan might be in trouble, Gates had sent in reinforcements. Leading the way was Benedict Arnold who rode back and forth among the American units, organizing men and encouraging them to fight.

Morgan's sharpshooters took the Redcoats by surprise during the first Battle of Saratoga.

Women at War

While only a handful of women actually fought in the Revolutionary War, both sides had female camp followers. These women traveled with the troops, cooking, washing clothes, and working as nurses. Major General Riedesel's wife, Frederika, was one of the camp followers at Saratoga. She kept a journal that has provided historians with important information about the battles and life in the British camp. After the first Battle of Saratoga she wrote, *"I saw the whole battle myself, and, knowing that my husband was taking part in it, I was filled with fear and anguish and shivered whenever a shot was fired."*

By this point Burgoyne's troops had arranged themselves into position at Freeman's Farm, and the two sides waged a full-scale battle. As artillery roared, each side tried to get a better position than its enemy. The Americans did not have any cannons on the field, but they were able to send more reinforcements into the thick of the fighting. As the battle raged back and forth, British cannons were captured and recaptured in fierce, close fighting and hand-to-hand combat. Morgan's riflemen rallied and set themselves up in the woods, even climbing trees to get better shots. These sharpshooters took a terrible toll on British soldiers.

When the fighting slowed, cries of the wounded and dying filled the air. Soon the exchange of gunfire erupted again. American Brigadier General John Glover said that "both armies seemed determined to conquer or die." At one point an American took aim at Burgoyne sitting on his horse. The bullet missed him and instead killed an officer who was bringing the general a message.

Late in the afternoon, Burgoyne had Riedesel enter the combat. Meanwhile, Arnold pleaded with Gates to send in more troops. After a heated argument, Gates ordered Arnold off the battlefield. When the Germans arrived on the scene with more cannons, the Americans were forced from the field.

The fighting lasted until dusk when the Americans finally retreated. After the long day's clash, 65 Americans lay dead on the battlefield, and another 250 or so were wounded or missing. The British could claim a victory of sorts since they controlled the battlefield, but they had paid an even higher price in casualties: 160 dead and more than 400 wounded or missing. The Americans had showed bravery that the British had not expected. Some British soldiers still had trouble accepting the American "rebels" as worthy enemies, but the fighting at Freeman's Farm helped changed that opinion.

After the Battle

Even with his losses, Burgoyne considered attacking again the next day. But his officers said their troops were too tired to fight, and he accepted their decision.

The Battle of Freeman's Farm

	American Army	British Army
Number of troops*:	8,300	7,500
Casualties:	315+	560+
Captured:	23	41

*Note: Neither army committed all of its troops in the battle.

The Americans were also exhausted, but they woke up on the morning of September 20 ready to fight. A British deserter warned the Americans that the British were planning to attack, but the assault never came. This was lucky for the Americans because the Northern Army was almost out of the lead balls they fired from their muskets. Gates sent an urgent message to Albany that his men needed more ammunition. Townspeople ripped metal strips out of window frames, melted them down into balls, and sent them to Bemis Heights.

Along with dwindling ammunition, Gates also had to face an angry Benedict Arnold. In his report of the battle at Freeman's Farm, Gates never mentioned Arnold by name, despite his undeniable bravery. Insulted, Arnold requested permission to leave the army to travel to Philadelphia to speak to Congress. Gates granted his request, but on the advice of fellow officers, Arnold decided to remain with the army.

Good News for the Patriots

While Arnold and Gates argued, the Americans received good news. To the north, American forces had attacked Fort Ticonderoga, capturing outer fortifications and two companies of British soldiers. They then headed southwest down Lake George and captured Fort George from the British. There they seized several hundred boats, which meant that Burgoyne's men would have an even harder time receiving supplies from Canada.

Burgoyne had some good news of his own. On September 21 he received a letter from General Henry Clinton, who commanded the British troops in New York City.

Clinton said that he could send 2,000 troops to help Burgoyne, but he didn't plan to have them go all the way to Albany. Instead, they would attack Fort Montgomery about 100 miles (161 km) south of Albany. Still, Burgoyne was thrilled with the news. He replied to Clinton, "An attack … upon Montgomery … will draw away a part of [the American] force … Do it, my dear friend, directly."

Burgoyne still hoped Clinton's men would go all the way to Albany. He waited patiently for word of Clinton's movement up the Hudson, but none came. He also learned that American forces had defeated some of the British troops his men were counting on to send them supplies.

Burgoyne's army was running out of food. American patrols had made it too dangerous for his men to go very far from their camp. During this time many British and German soldiers deserted. Burgoyne angrily threatened that his American Indian allies would scalp any man captured while trying to run away.

By early October Clinton had finally left New York City with 3,000 men. After they seized two forts on the Hudson River, Clinton tried to send the news to Burgoyne by inserting a message inside a silver bullet and giving it to a spy. But the Americans captured the spy, who swallowed the bullet. His captors forced him to take medicine that made him throw up the bullet. As a result, Burgoyne didn't learned of Clinton's victory until much later.

Meanwhile, even with his forces hungry and greatly outnumbered, Burgoyne was eager to fight again. At Bemis Heights, Gates and his army waited. He was sure that the British would launch one more attack.

Secret Messages

Generals Clinton and Burgoyne often wrote each other notes using a special code. To send a message, one of the men wrote sentences that said nothing important. But they had to choose their words carefully because certain words in each sentence held the real message. The receiver knew which words those were by putting the letter under a special piece of paper called a "mask," which had a hole in the shape of an hourglass or the number 8 cut out. The words within the cutout held the real message. If the Americans captured the message, they wouldn't see the secret message inside the larger letter unless they had an exact copy of the mask.

You will have heard, Dr Sir I doubt not long before this can have reached you that **Sir W. Howe** is gone from hence. The Rebels imagine that he **is gone to the** Eastward. By this time however he has filled **Chesapeak bay with** surprize and terror.

Washington marched **the greater part of the** Rebels to Philadelphia in order to oppose Sir Wm's. **army. I hear he is** now returned upon finding none of our troops **landed but am not** sure of this, great part of his troops are returned for **certain. I am** sure this countermarching must be ruin to them. I am **left to command** here, half of my force may I am sure defend everything **here with** much safety. I shall therefore send Sir W. 4 or 5 Batns. I have **too small a force** to invade the New England provinces; they are too weak **to make any effectual** efforts against me and you do not want any **diversion in your favour.** I can, therefore very well spare him 1500 men. **I shall try some thing** certainly towards the close of the year, not till then **at any rate. It may be of use** to inform you that report says all yields **to you. I own to you that I think** the business will quickly be over now. **Sr. W's move just at this time** has been capital. Washington's have been **the worst he could take** in every respect. sincerely give you **much joy on your success** and am with great Sincerity your [ ] HC

CHAPTER *Four*

A Great Victory

Even with his men outnumbered and hungry, Burgoyne thought he could take on the Americans at Bemis Heights.

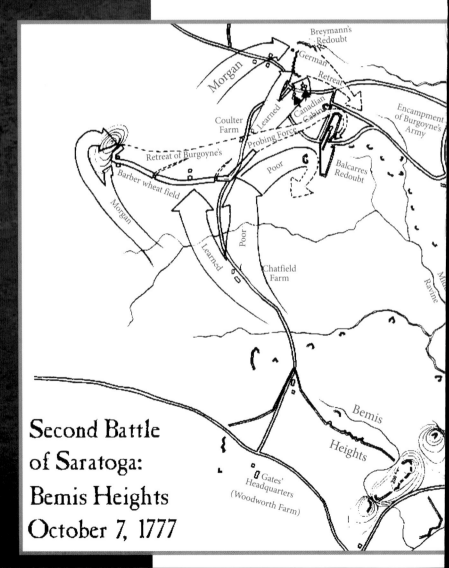

Second Battle of Saratoga: Bemis Heights October 7, 1777

He knew he couldn't retreat without risking being caught by the larger American force. He also could not establish a new, secure way to get supplies from Canada. He hoped that Clinton would arrive soon with reinforcements, and together they could still take Albany.

At Bemis Heights on the morning of October 7, Gates sent Colonel James Wilkinson to scout the situation. From the woods around the heights, Wilkinson could see British troops harvesting wheat to make bread. Wilkinson also noticed several generals looking through their spyglasses. But from that distance, he couldn't tell if Burgoyne was one of them.

Wilkinson returned to camp and reported his findings to Gates, who prepared some of his men to meet the British. Around noon Gates heard gunfire nearby. The second Battle of Saratoga had begun.

"[O]rder on Morgan to begin the game."

—Horatio Gates, after receiving Wilkinson's report, signaling the start of the second Battle of Saratoga

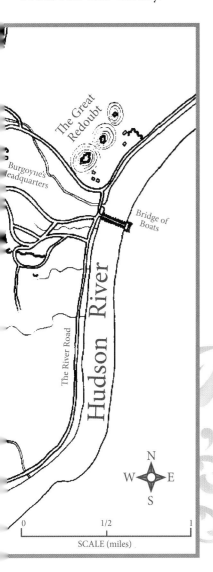

The Great Redoubt

Burgoyne's Headquarters

Bridge of Boats

The River Road

Hudson River

N
W E
S

0   1/2   1
SCALE (miles)

First Action of the Day

Shortly after the first shots rang out, Benedict Arnold volunteered to scout out the battle lines. Gates reluctantly agreed, but he sent General Benjamin Lincoln along to make sure that Arnold didn't do anything risky. When they returned, Arnold insisted, "You must send a strong force." Gates didn't like being told what to do, so he banned Arnold from taking part in the battle. Even so, Gates took Arnold's advice and sent out more troops under the command of General Enoch Poor.

The plan was to attack the enemy from two sides. Poor's men struck first from the east, as Morgan's men swung far to the west of the British column near the wheat field. The British saw groups of patriots moving through the woods but had no idea how many troops they faced. At times the British fired their cannons, but it didn't stop the Americans. When the Americans finally poured out of the forest, they struck hard, quickly killing about two dozen British soldiers. They also captured a cannon, which they turned around to fire on the retreating enemy.

At the other end of the field, Morgan's riflemen and some light infantrymen forced the British from their posts. Burgoyne tried to send word to another of his generals to swing into action, but the messenger was shot.

Back at the patriot camp, Arnold knew the battle was raging, and he wanted to be a part of it. He took a horse and charged toward the front lines. Gates sent an aide to bring him back, but he was unable to catch up to Arnold.

Storming the Redoubt

To the American soldiers at Bemis Heights, Arnold was a hero. They cheered as he reached them and stirred them to fight harder. They needed encouragement because they were attacking cannons head-on in the center of the British line and facing Germans who didn't give up easily. The success on the ends of the line, combined with Arnold's attack in the center caused Burgoyne's entire line to collapse.

Chaos gripped the smoke-filled battlefield, especially for the British. Officers watched as their men threw down their guns and ran off the battlefield. Some headed for a redoubt the British had built earlier. Some tried to shield themselves behind trees. Other British soldiers made a more orderly retreat.

At the Battle of Saratoga, patriot forces (in light blue) charged British and German troops who secured themselves behind a redoubt.

The arrival of several thousand additional patriot soldiers seemed to ensure an American victory. The Americans had driven the British from the battlefield, but Arnold was not ready to stop fighting. He led an assault on the larger of the two British redoubts.

The assault failed, but Arnold then joined with troops that were attacking the smaller and more exposed Breymann's Redoubt. Lieutenant Colonel Heinrich Breymann's outnumbered soldiers fired several rounds at the advancing Americans, but they

Benedict Arnold was shot in the leg at the Battle of Saratoga.

kept coming and overwhelmed their position. One shot killed Arnold's horse, and another struck the general in the left leg. American soldiers carried their wounded leader off the battlefield.

The Americans continued the assault and stormed over the redoubt's walls. Germans fled the small fort, while Breymann and several of his men lay dead inside. By losing control of the redoubt, Burgoyne's entire camp was threatened. Only darkness halted the Americans from completing their victory.

Hessian soldiers fled the scene when the Americans attacked them at Breymann's Redoubt.

During the two battles collectively known as the Battle of Saratoga, Burgoyne suffered heavy losses—about 1,200 men, including one of his favorite generals and closest friends, Simon Fraser, who was shot by one of Morgan's riflemen. The American losses were much lower, and Gates' army now outnumbered the British by about two to one. Still, American troops knew the pain of the battlefield. One Continental officer wrote that during the night, "the groans and shrieks of the wounded and dying, and the horrors of the whole scene baffle all description."

"That gallant officer is General Fraser. I admire him, but it is necessary he should die. Do your duty."

—Colonel Daniel Morgan, pointing out General Fraser to his sharpshooters

Seeking Peace

On the night of October 8, under the cover of darkness, Burgoyne and his men abandoned their wounded comrades and began a slow retreat up the Hudson River. Marching in a torrential downpour, it took Burgoyne's weary, defeated, and hungry troops nearly an entire day to march about 8 miles (13 km) to Saratoga (present-day Schuylerville). That night, his remaining troops were so tired they didn't even have the strength to chop firewood.

Gates' army followed Burgoyne and his men to Saratoga. When the Americans arrived on October 10, Burgoyne and his forces dug in to defend themselves. Gates' army gradually surrounded Burgoyne's troops and blocked all avenues of escape.

At the same time, more militiamen arrived to bolster the American force, which continuously bombarded Burgoyne's army. More of his Indian allies and professional soldiers deserted.

Burgoyne met with his surviving officers on October 13. Together they decided to surrender to Gates. Burgoyne had no idea that General Henry Clinton was about to send about 1,700 troops up the Hudson to help him. By the time those forces began their mission on October 15, Gates and Burgoyne were already working out the details of a surrender. And in the end, those troops would not have been able to help Burgoyne. Clinton eventually called them back because his army was ordered to go to Philadelphia to defend the capital.

The Battle of Bemis Heights

	American Army	British Army
Number of troops*:	13,000	6,800
Casualties:	150	450
Captured:	5	180

*Note: Neither army committed all of its troops in the battle.

Still, the presence of the reinforcements on the Hudson worried Gates. He didn't know how many men Clinton had sent, so he wanted the peace talks to go as quickly as possible. But the talks were slowed because the two generals did not meet face to face. Instead, staff officers met and negotiated the terms of surrender.

Gates started the talks by demanding that the British surrender unconditionally. All of Burgoyne's troops would become prisoners of war, and they would be stripped of their weapons.

Insulted by Gates' demands, Burgoyne wrote back with his own proposal. In the end the generals agreed upon a generous set of terms. Burgoyne's army was to surrender the property of the king, including muskets, cannons, and flags. The officers and soldiers could keep their private property. Then they would march to Boston where they would board ships for Europe. Although free, they would promise not to fight again in North America during the present war. The whole agreement was not even called a surrender; it was known as the Convention of Saratoga.

Burgoyne was surprised that Gates quickly agreed to these terms and wanted the surrender signed as soon as possible. Burgoyne sensed that Gates knew some of Clinton's men were on their way north. Noting Gates' desire for speed, Burgoyne wanted to drag out the talks to give his supposed rescuers more time to arrive.

That night a loyalist came to Burgoyne's camp with news of the reinforcements going up the Hudson. Burgoyne asked his officers if it would be wrong of him to break the deal he had made with Gates. Most of them said yes.

Still, Burgoyne wanted to delay signing the treaty. He questioned Gates about some of the terms and wanted to be able to count how many men were in the American camp. Burgoyne had agreed to surrender thinking he was vastly outnumbered. He claimed he had received a report that many of the American soldiers had left Bemis Heights. If that were true, then the British might still be able to fight their way out. Gates flatly refused this request, and he gave Burgoyne an hour deadline to sign the agreement or the Americans would attack. Burgoyne signed. The campaign now known as the Battle of Saratoga was officially over.

Did You Know?

As Burgoyne handed over his sword in surrender to American General Horatio Gates, he said, "The fortunes of war have made me your prisoner." Gates gallantly replied, "I shall always be ready to testify that it was through no fault of your excellency."

CHAPTER *Five*

A Turning Point

On the morning of October 17, 1777, drummers once again played in Burgoyne's camp. But this time, instead of calling men to battle, the drums signaled the end of a long campaign.

The meeting between the two generals was pleasant. Gates assured Burgoyne that he wouldn't tell anyone that he was to blame for the British loss. Gates truly believed what he said. Many events beyond Burgoyne's control had led to the British defeat near Saratoga.

As the generals chatted, about 6,000 British and German soldiers marched toward an old fort where they left their guns in huge piles. Then they waited to begin their long march to Boston and their journey home. Gates had ordered his men to keep quiet and refrain from

British soldiers marched through the American camp when General Burgoyne formally surrendered to General Gates.

insulting the enemy after their defeat. Burgoyne's soldiers were grateful that the Americans did not taunt or jeer.

A Friendly Surrender

The two generals dined together that night, and Burgoyne noted the one major advantage Gates had during the campaign: While Burgoyne saw his forces dwindle over time, Gates' only grew, as more militia rushed to join the American cause.

After dinner Gates offered to get Burgoyne a ship that would immediately take him back to England. Burgoyne declined, saying that he would wait for the official word from General Howe.

The Continental Congress did not like the terms of surrender between Gates and Burgoyne. Among other things, they feared that the British government would send the soldiers back to fight the

Americans. As a result, they were in no hurry to ship Burgoyne's soldiers home.

In early 1778 Burgoyne wrote a letter to Congress complaining

When Burgoyne met with Gates to formally surrender, it was not their first meeting. They had once served in the same regiment decades before when both were young officers in the British Army.

about delays in returning his army to Britain. Congress used the letter to cancel the Convention, which essentially made Burgoyne and his men prisoners of war. Burgoyne was allowed to return to Britain, but his soldiers remained in the United States until they were released in a prisoner exchange later in the war.

After the Fighting Stopped

The victory at Saratoga was the greatest achievement of Gates' career, and he hoped even more would come of it. He talked about leading an invasion of Canada. Privately, he also discussed the possibility of becoming commander in chief of the Continental army. George Washington had been criticized for losing the battles that allowed the British to take Philadelphia. To members of Congress who liked Gates—or disliked Washington—Saratoga proved that Gates was a better general. But Gates still had political and military enemies. Some noted that unlike Burgoyne and Arnold, Gates had never gotten close to the battlefield. And under enemy fire, it was Arnold who organized troops and urged them to keep fighting, not Gates.

Ultimately, Gates did not have enough supporters to take Washington's job, but he was made a member of the new Board of War. This group managed the war effort, and in a way, it controlled Washington's actions.

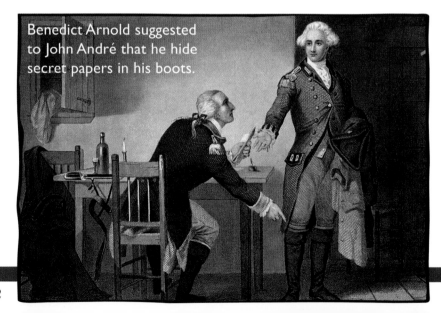

Benedict Arnold suggested to John André that he hide secret papers in his boots.

The Treason of Benedict Arnold

Benedict Arnold had fought bravely at Saratoga as he had throughout the war. But he felt that members of Congress and some generals, including Horatio Gates, had never given him the respect he deserved. In 1780, when Arnold took command of the American fort at West Point, he decided to betray his country. In addition to his anger over how he had been treated, Arnold was also in debt. In exchange for about 6,000 British pounds (more than $1 million today), he agreed to help the British capture West Point.

Arnold and Major John André, a British officer, set their plan into motion in September 1780. In disguise, André met with Arnold at West Point but was captured as he tried to return to British lines. Arnold knew that papers André was carrying in his boots described their plot, so he fled to a British ship before the Americans could capture him. Soon he was leading loyalist forces against patriots. One raid destroyed New London, Connecticut, just a few miles from where he was born.

After the war Arnold lived in Canada and England, where he died at age 60. All across the United States, he was despised as a traitor. The name Benedict Arnold became a synonym for "treachery" or "treason." His name is still used as an insult against someone who betrays a country or cause. With his reputation as a patriot hero tarnished, Arnold's bravery at the Battle of Saratoga has all but been forgotten.

Meanwhile, Arnold was still healing from his battlefield wound. Although he was unable to return to battle, he was named military commander in Philadelphia in June 1778. The British had held the city only a few months before deciding to pull out. The loss at Saratoga played a significant role in their decision.

France Enters the War

In November 1777 rumors of the loss of Philadelphia to the British reached Benjamin Franklin in Paris. A few weeks later the news was confirmed. But along with the bad news came the good. The messenger told Franklin, "But sir, I have greater news than that: General Burgoyne and his whole army are prisoners of war!" Franklin and the others quickly spread the good news. They told Congress that the French reaction was as if "it had been a victory of their own troops over their own enemies." The victory at Saratoga convinced the French that the young United States had the military might to win its independence. France was ready to offer its full support to the American cause.

French and American diplomats signed two treaties on February 6, 1778. These treaties officially recognized the United States as an independent nation and established trade relations between the two countries. France also agreed to enter the war against Britain to make sure the United States remained independent.

For the British, war with France was terrible news. King George III would have to send ships and men across the entire British empire to defend its colonies. And the British could not rule out attacks on Great Britain itself. They would also have less money to spend on the war in North America.

In 1778 France agreed to help the United States fight for independence from Great Britain.

Even so, King George wanted to continue fighting despite growing opposition to the war among members of Parliament. As a result, the British decided to focus on regaining control of the southern states. They assumed that they could count on more support from the loyalists there than they had gotten in the North. With that help, they could use fewer of their own troops.

For the Americans, when they heard about the treaty with France in May 1778, it stirred in them joy and hope for a quick victory.

Washington's army at Valley Forge celebrated by firing cannons and shouting, "Long live the king of France!"

"I believe no event was ever received with a more heartfelt joy."
—George Washington, May 1, 1778, after hearing the news of the treaty with France

The situation grew even worse for the British when Spain entered the war in 1779. Although Spain did not send troops to the United States as France did, it did send money. The Netherlands was also pulled into the war. The conflict spilled over into Central America, the Caribbean, Asia, and Africa.

But the war did not end as quickly as some Americans had hoped. Small battles continued along the Hudson River and in other parts of the North. In the South, major battles took place in the Carolinas before the fighting moved to Virginia. There, in October 1781, a fleet of French ships and several thousand soldiers helped Washington and his troops defeat the British at Yorktown. With that loss, Parliament decided to end the war.

When John Burgoyne drew up his plan to invade New York, he thought the campaign would help end the war. And it did—just not in the way he had hoped. Instead, the U.S. victories at Saratoga helped pave the way for America's victory and independence.

The British surrendered to the Americans at the Battle of Yorktown—the last major battle of the Revolutionary War.

April 19, 1775: The Revolutionary War begins.

June 17, 1777: British General John Burgoyne begins his campaign southward from Canada.

July 5, 1777: American defenders abandon Fort Ticonderoga, New York.

July 7, 1777: During the Battle of Hubbardton in Vermont, the patriots offer stiff resistance, but ultimately end up retreating into the woods.

July 8, 1777: After a fierce battle that the Americans nearly won, they set fire to Fort Ann in New York and retreat to Fort Edward.

August 6, 1777: The British and their Indian allies defeat the Americans at the Battle of Oriskany.

August 16, 1777: Under the command of General John Stark, American militia win the Battle of Bennington.

August 19, 1777: General Horatio Gates takes command of the Northern Army in New York.

September 19, 1777: The first Battle of Saratoga takes place at Freeman's Farm with the British driving the Americans off the field but suffering more casualties.

October 3, 1777: British General Henry Clinton begins his diversionary attack in the southern Hudson Valley.

October 6, 1777: Clinton's troops overrun and capture Forts Clinton and Montgomery.

October 7, 1777: The Americans win the second Battle of Saratoga at Bemis Heights.

October 8, 1777: Burgoyne retreats northward.

October 10, 1777: Gates' army catches up to Burgoyne at Saratoga.

October 10–14, 1777: The Americans surround and bombard Burgoyne's army at Saratoga.

October 14, 1777: Burgoyne asks for terms of surrender.

October 15–16, 1777: Negotiations between the two armies result in the Convention of Saratoga.

October 17, 1777: Burgoyne formally surrenders to Gates at Saratoga.

February 6, 1778: France and the United States sign treaties in which France promises to help the Americans win their independence from Great Britain.

October 1781: French soldiers and ships play a huge role in defeating the British at Yorktown, Virginia; the loss convinces Great Britain to end the war.

April 11, 1783: The Revolutionary War officially ends.

Glossary

ambush—a surprise attack

artillery—large guns, such as cannons, that require several soldiers to load, aim, and fire

bayonet—a long metal blade attached to the end of a musket or rifle

breastworks—temporary fortifications used during a battle

casualties—people killed, wounded, or missing in a battle or war

deserter—a military member who leaves duty without permission

diplomat—someone who deals with other nations to create or maintain good relationships

diversion—something that takes attention away from what is happening

Hessian—a German soldier hired by the British

infantryman—a soldier trained, armed, and equipped to fight on foot

loyalist—a colonist who was loyal to Great Britain during the Revolutionary War

militia—a group of volunteer citizens organized to fight but who are not professional soldiers

Parliament—the national legislature of Great Britain

patriot—a person who sided with the American Colonies during the Revolutionary War

rear guard—a group of soldiers who are placed at the back of an army to protect it from being attacked from behind

redoubt—a small building or area that gives protection to soldiers under attack

reinforcement—extra troops sent into battle

siege—placement of an army around a location in order to cut off its supplies and force its surrender

skirmish—a small battle

spyglass—a small telescope that makes faraway objects appear larger and closer

treachery—breaking or betraying of trust; disloyal behavior

Further Reading

Burgan, Michael. *The Split History of the American Revolution.* North Mankato, Minn: Compass Point Books, 2013.

Clarke, Gordon. *Significant Battles of the American Revolution.* New York: Crabtree Publishing Company, 2013.

Kent, Deborah. *The American Revolution: From Bunker Hill to Yorktown.* Berkeley Heights, N.J.: Enslow Publishers, 2011.

Raum, Elizabeth. *True Stories of the Revolutionary War.* North Mankato, Minn: Capstone Press, 2013.

Sheinkin, Steve. *The Notorious Benedict Arnold: A True Story of Adventure, Heroism & Treachery.* New York: Roaring Brook Press, 2010.

Internet Sites

Use FactHound to find Internet sites related to this book. All of the sites on FactHound have been researched by our staff.

Here's all you do:

Visit *www.facthound.com*

Type in this code: 9780756549749

Critical Thinking Using the Common Core

1. The Battle of Saratoga has been called a turning point in the Revolutionary War. Use evidence from the text to support this claim. (Key Ideas and Details)

2. Do you think Benedict Arnold was justified in switching his loyalties to the British? How might he have handled the situation differently? Write an argument to support your claim using logical reasoning and relevant evidence from the text. (Text Types and Purposes)

Source Notes

Page 7, col. 1, line 5: Philander D. Chase, ed. *The Papers of George Washington, Revolutionary War Series, vol 7. 12, 21 October 1776–5 January 1777.* Charlottesville: University Press of Virginia, 1997, pp. 289–292.

Page 7, col. 2, line 3: Thomas Fleming. *Liberty!: The American Revolution.* New York: Viking, 1997, p. 224.

Page 9, callout quote: Max M. Mintz. *The Generals of Saratoga: John Burgoyne & Horatio Gates.* New Haven: Yale University Press, 1990, p. 55.

Page 13, col. 1, line 10: Henry Steele Commager and Richard B. Morris, eds. *The Spirit of 'Seventy-Six: The Story of the American Revolution as Told by Participants.* New York: Harper & Row, 1967, p. 548.

Page 14, fact box, line 6: *The Spirit of 'Seventy-Six*, p. 546.

Page 15, col. 1, line 3: Richard M. Ketchum. *Saratoga: The Turning Point of America's Revolutionary War.* New York: H. Holt, 1997, p. 162.

Page 23, col. 2, line 3: *The Spirit of 'Seventy-Six*, p. 572.

Page 33, sidebar, line 8: "Baroness on the Battlefield." *American Heritage.* December 1964, Vol. 16, issue 1.

Page 33, col. 2, line 10: *Saratoga: The Turning Point of America's Revolutionary War*, p. 363.

Page 36, col. 1, line 9: *History of the Proceedings and Debates of the House of Commons*, Vol. 7, p. 246.

Page 39, callout quote: General James Wilkinson. *Memoirs of My Own Times*, Vol. 1. Printed by Abraham Small, 1816, p. 268.

Page 40, col. 1, line 9: *Saratoga: The Turning Point of America's Revolutionary War*, p. 394.

Page 44, col. 1, line 15: *The Spirit of 'Seventy-Six*, p. 595.

Page 44, callout quote: Joel Tyler Headley. *Washington and His Generals,* Vol. 1. New York: Baker and Scribner, 1847, p. 273.

Page 47, fact box, line 3: "Liberty! The American Revolution: Saratoga 1777." 29 Oct. 2014. http://www.pbs.org/ktca/liberty/chronicle_saratoga1777.html

Page 54, col. 1, line 8: *Liberty!: The American Revolution*, p. 269.

Page 54, col. 1, line 14: *Saratoga: The Turning Point of America's Revolutionary War*, p. 445.

Page 56, callout quote: *Official Letters to the Honorable American Congress from George Washington*, Vol. 2, 1795, p. 273.

Select Bibliography

Boatner, Mark M. III. *Encyclopedia of the American Revolution*. Mechanicsburg, Pa.: Stackpole Books, 1994.

"British Execution of the Campaign of 1777." Worcester Polytechnic Institute. July 22, 2014. http://www.wpi.edu/academics/military/absexe1777.html

Cogliano, Francis D. *Revolutionary America, 1763–1815: A Political History*. London: Routledge, 2009.

Commager, Henry Steele and Richard B. Morris, eds. *The Spirit of 'Seventy-Six: The Story of the American Revolution as Told by Participants*. New York: Harper & Row, 1967.

Corbett, Theodore. *No Turning Point: The Saratoga Campaign in Perspective*. Norman, Okla.: University of Oklahoma Press, 2012.

Fleming, Thomas. *Liberty!: The American Revolution*. New York: Viking, 1997.

Ketchum, Richard M. *Saratoga: The Turning Point of America's Revolutionary War*. New York: H. Holt, 1997.

Mintz, Max M. *The Generals of Saratoga: John Burgoyne & Horatio Gates*. New Haven, Conn.: Yale University Press, 1990.

"Saratoga: The Tide Turns on the Frontier." National Park Service. 21 July 2014. http://www.nps.gov/nr/twhp/wwwlps/lessons/93saratoga/93saratoga.htm

Stewart, Richard W., ed. *American Military History*. Vol. 1. Washington, D.C.: Center of Military History. U.S. Army, 2005. http://www.history.army.mil/books/AMH-V1/ch04.htm

"The 1777 Siege of Fort Schuyler." Fort Stanwix National Monument. http://www.nps.gov/fost/historyculture/the-1777-siege-of-fort-schuyler.htm

Index

About the Author

Michael Burgan has written more than 250 books for children and teens, mostly on U.S. history. He specializes in the Colonial era and the period just before and after the American Revolution. Michael lives in Santa Fe, New Mexico.